MOVIE DUETS FOR ALL

Playable on ANY TWO INSTRUMENTS
or any number of instruments in ensemble

Arranged by Michael Story

Alfred

ISBN-10: 0-7390-6307-3
ISBN-13: 978-0-7390-6307-1

DOUBLE TROUBLE
(From "Harry Potter and The Prisoner of Azkaban" - 2004)

B♭ TRUMPET/BARITONE T.C.

Very bright "4" or moderate "2"

Music by **JOHN WILLIAMS**
Arranged by MICHAEL STORY

*A♯ = B♭

33518

IN DREAMS
(From "The Lord of the Rings: The Fellowship of the Ring" - 2001)

Words and Music by
FRAN WALSH and HOWARD SHORE
Arranged by MICHAEL STORY

33518

SINGIN' IN THE RAIN
(From "Singin' in the Rain" - 1952)

Music by NACIO HERB BROWN
Arranged by MICHAEL STORY

THE ENTERTAINER
(From Various Movies)

By SCOTT JOPLIN
Arranged by MICHAEL STORY

TWISTIN' THE NIGHT AWAY
(From "Animal House" - 1978 and "Innerspace" - 1987)

Words and Music by
SAM COOKE
Arranged by MICHAEL STORY

Bright rock shuffle

33518

WE'RE OFF TO SEE THE WIZARD
(From "The Wizard of Oz" - 1939)

Music by HAROLD ARLEN
Arranged by MICHAEL STORY

*A♯ = B♭

BE OUR GUEST
(From "Beauty and the Beast" - 1991)

Lyrics by HOWARD ASHMAN
Music by ALAN MENKEN
Arranged by MICHAEL STORY

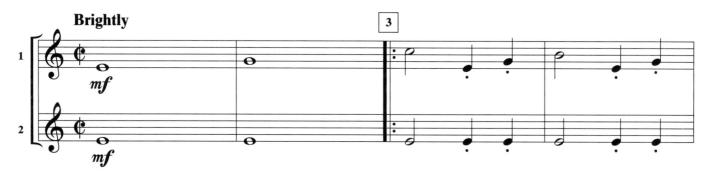

FAME
(From "Fame" - 1980, 2009)

Music by
MICHAEL GORE
Arranged by MICHAEL STORY

WONKA'S WELCOME SONG
(From "Charlie and the Chocolate Factory" - 2005)

Music by
DANNY ELFMAN
Arranged by MICHAEL STORY

WIZARD WHEEZES
(From "Harry Potter and the Half-Blood Prince" - 2009)

By NICHOLAS HOOPER
Arranged by MICHAEL STORY

*A♯ = B♭
**D♯ = E♭

CAN YOU READ MY MIND?
Love Theme
(From "Superman" - 1978)

Music by **JOHN WILLIAMS**
Arranged by MICHAEL STORY

STAR WARS
Main Title
(From the "Star Wars" Series – 1977-2005)

Music by **JOHN WILLIAMS**
Arranged by MICHAEL STORY

(EVERYTHING I DO) I DO IT FOR YOU
(From "Robin Hood: Prince of Thieves" - 1991)

Words and Music by BRYAN ADAMS,
ROBERT JOHN "MUTT" LANGE and MICHAEL KAMEN
Arranged by MICHAEL STORY

I DON'T WANT TO MISS A THING
(From "Armageddon" - 1998 and "Dragon Ball Z: Return of Cooler" - 2002)

Words and Music by
DIANE WARREN
Arranged by MICHAEL STORY

33518

LIVING IN AMERICA
(From "Rocky IV" - 1985)

Words and Music by
DAN HARTMAN and CHARLIE MIDNIGHT
Arranged by MICHAEL STORY

GONNA FLY NOW
(From the "Rocky" Series – 1976-2006)

Words and Music by
BILL CONTI, AYN ROBBINS and CAROL CONNORS
Arranged by MICHAEL STORY

THEME FROM "SUPERMAN"
(From the "Superman" Series – 1978-2006)

Music by
JOHN WILLIAMS
Arranged by MICHAEL STORY

Majestic march

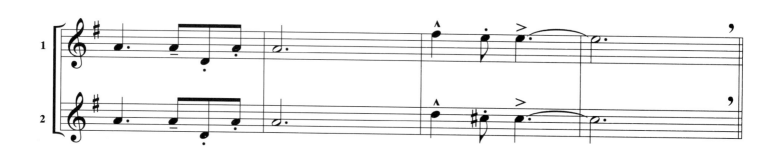

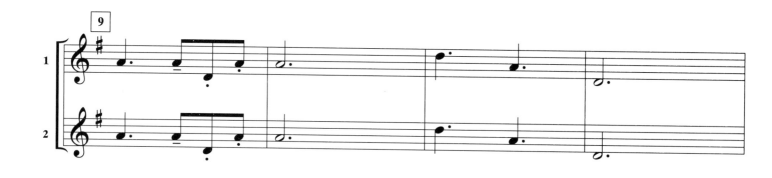